Gerome's Magical Garden

Read, Plant, Grow
A Magical Garden Adventure for Children

Created by Greg Raleigh • Written by Edna Perkins • Illustrated by Kris Gausman

© 2010 Enchanting Gnome Knowledge, Inc., LLC
All rights reserved.

No part of this publication may be reproduced, or stored in a retrieval system, or transmitted in any form or by any means, electronic, mechanical, photocopying, recording, or otherwise, without written permission of the publisher.

ISBN 978-0-578-05407-0

Enchanting Gnome Knowledge, Inc.
E7970 640th Avenue
Elk Mound, WI 54739

gerome@geromethegnome.com

www.geromethegnome.com

To my loving wife, Michele, and to my niece, Rachel, for their unwavering support.
– Greg Raleigh

To my beautiful daughter-in-law, Katie, whom I love as my own. To my loving husband, Tim, who said, "Why not?"
And to my inquisitive and wonderful son, TJ, who was the first to ask me to write him a story.
– Edna Perkins

In memory of my mother, Audrey, whom I watched paint in soft colors,
and to my daughter, Hannah, who paints my life in bright colors.
– Kris Gausman

20 19 18 17 16 15 14 13 12 11 10   1 2 3 4 5 6 7 8 9 10

Printed in Chippewa Falls, Wisconsin. First printing April 2010.

This book is printed on paper that contains 10 percent post-consumer waste and that is produced in accordance with certifications that ensure responsible forest management. It is also printed using low-solvent, low-voc vegetable-based ink.

The illustrations in this book were done in colored pencil on Mylar.

Hear Ye! Hear Ye!

A Royal Message from Gerome, King of the Gnomes

By my royal decree as King of the Gnomes,
I share the Secret Gnome History.

Gnomes appeared many years ago when magical and wise unicorns looked after the Earth. Gnomes were granted the honor of becoming Keepers of the Earth Gardens by the unicorns and were chosen because of their gentleness, kindness, and love of the earth.

During childhood, each gnome must make a journey to the home of the unicorns to create a magical staff woven from a unicorn's mane. The gnomes use their magical staffs to call the creatures of the earth and sky to help care for gardens.

Turn the pages of this book to reveal magical garden secrets and more Gnome Knowledge scrolls. Join me and my friends for a wonderful garden adventure.

His Kind and Generous,

Gerome, King of the Gnomes

In every house there is a gnome,
> deeply sleeping in his warm and cozy home.

Waiting and waiting…
> For what, you ask?
> > Why, for you,
> > > don't you know?

Shhh… now listen carefully.
> There is magic in the hearts
> of gnomes, you see.

Gnome Knowledge
Gnomes live all over the world and are magical creatures who tend to Earth's gardens.

To wake your very own magic gnome,
 you must do these things on your own.

Take your trowel
 and TAP! TAP! TAP!
 Then shout out loud,
 "Gerome, I want to plant!"

Are you ready?
 TAP! TAP! TAP!
 "GEROME, I WANT TO PLANT!"

You did it,
   you did it,
      you marvelous child!

Gerome the Gnome has come to your home!

   "Hello, my dear little one!
      How do you do?
         Plant, you say?
            Let's make a garden today!"

In Gerome's hand, he holds his magical staff,
   with a hearty gnome laugh
      and a mighty TAP! TAP! TAP!

Up hops a friendly frog named Freddie.
   He is Gerome's silly sidekick,
      so helpful and ready.

So eager to plant, so willing to reap,
   up he goes with a glorious leap.

Skippity dippity
Freddie goes.

Hoppity
boppity,
to and fro.

Gnome Knowledge

Frogs prefer to be in cool, moist conditions under leafy plants, where they find insects to eat. Frogs catch insects with their long, sticky tongues. This makes frogs wonderful garden friends.

Then with another mighty TAP! TAP! TAP!
from below Earth's deep and hidden map,
the Gnome King calls beloved Queen Terra.
Away we go with our trusty friends,
to plant a garden by this day's end.

Gnome Knowledge

Worms tunnel deep into gardens to mix the dirt. Earthworms have sticky slime on them that contains an important food for plants called nitrogen. The sticky slime also helps to hold clumps of dirt together.

We turn the dirt over and must not forget
the delightful compost to feed and protect.
With a magical zing and a heavenly rain shower,
our plants will grow as big as a tower.

Gnome Knowledge

Compost is plant or food scraps such as leaves, grass clippings, and coffee grounds. Compost is good because it provides food for the Earth and helps recycle our food scraps.

For each little seed, we make a comfy, cozy bed
where each will lay its tiny, sweet head.

Gently we cover each little seed.
A blanket of dirt is what it will need.

A marker is placed at each tidy row.
We don't want to forget what grows below.

Look at the snuggly home we have made.
Soon we'll see veggies from seeds we have laid.

Gnome Knowledge
When planting seeds, remember that the larger the seed, the deeper it should be planted. Some very small seeds are scattered directly on the soil and not covered up at all. Read any seed packet you buy to find the correct depth.

Great Gnome Magic tends our seedlings.
>   We share in the watering and also the feeding.

Soon tiny sprouts will be popping out.
>   Then we will give a joyful shout!

Mr. Sun is nodding to sleep.
Our shadows are growing long and deep.

Off we go to our beds,
where we will lay our weary heads.

Now Mr. Moon's glow covers the land.
What a joy it has been to give Gerome a hand.

Our sweet seeds are slumbering in their home.
Good night, my dear Gerome the Gnome.

Color Your Garden Friends

Wake up, wake up,
   my dear little children!
      Spring up, spring up,
         dear sleepy, sweet seedlings.

Gerome, the King of Gnomes,
   has now proclaimed,
"'Tis the season of growing."

A garden secret is about to unfold.
So, come, dear children, listen well.
It's a gift from Gerome. Do tell! Do tell!

With a wise wink and a happy heart,
   Gerome is ready, so let us start.

First we ask for a full rain cloud
　　to gently drop water
　　　　down,
　　　　　　down,
　　　　　　　　down,
　　　　　　　　　　where our seeds can be found,
　　　　　　　　　　　　deep in beds underground.

Then we ask for cheery sunlight
  to warm the earth and tickle our seeds
    with great delight!

The seeds will wiggle and soon begin to jiggle.

Peeking up from their beds,
  bright green sprouts will stretch and yawn,
    up and smiling with the dawn.

A TAP! TAP! TAP!
from the magical staff.
Queen Terra pops out with a
giggle and a laugh.

Tender sprout roots need air and water.
In and out, squirmy wormies will go,
making paths deep down under
and helping plants to grow and grow.

Gnome Knowledge

Worms are essential to the survival of plant life. They make tunnels that create a path for water and air to provide nourishment to the roots.

Children, take heed.
> Beware of the nasty weed.
>> Pluck and pull this unruly pest.
>>> Our gnome friends will do the rest.

Look at our sweet peas growing taller!
Our next task is to make sure
they don't fall over.
Let us begin by picking up sticks.
A sturdy trellis is what we will fix.

What sticks will we pick?
Why, long straight sticks.
One is here.
One is there.
Place one here.
Place one there.
Snip it here.
Tie it there.

Rising toward the great blue sky
comes crazy Razzy Radish.
His joy is flying high!
Oh, so snazzy, red, and jazzy.

Mmm, delish!

Sprawling Luscious Linda Lettuce
is looking lovely as can be.
Her tasty leaves are green and tender.
Our job is to keep her trim
and slender.

Freddie leaps with joyful glee,
for weaving in and out
is gentle, sprouting Sweet Pea.
Join them with a happy shout!

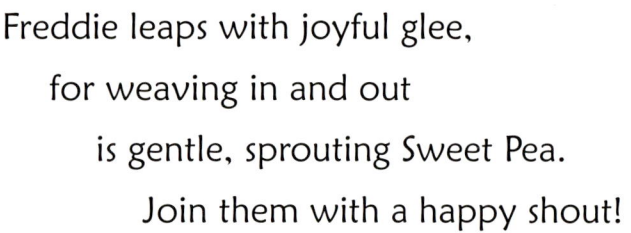

Big Ben has sweet bean flowers
growing up like bushy towers
and basking in the sun's warm light.
It's a stunning and delightful sight!

Gnome Knowledge

The part of the carrot that we eat comes from the root system. Plants such as carrots have a single large root for storing nutrients.

Up from the ground and stretching tall
comes Carl Carrot's great big top.
With an orange root,
so yummy to all.
Such a cute and crunchy crop!

Look at her grow, Silly Sally Spinach!
This is a veggie you will want to finish.
She'll make you strong
to play all day long.

Listen… TAP! TAP! TAP!

   What was that?

Then a mighty RAP! RAP! RAP!

   Can you hear that?

Bzzz… Bzzz… Bzzz…

   "Thelma Sue, I am calling you!"

    shouts the mighty King of Gnomes.

"We're buzzy bees, ready to please. Bzzz, Bzzz, Bzzz,"

   says dear Queen Thelma Sue. "Bzzz, Bzzz, Bzzz."

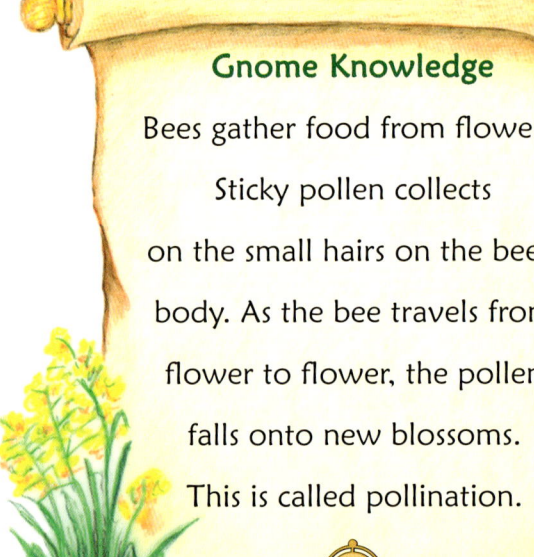

Gnome Knowledge

Bees gather food from flowers. Sticky pollen collects on the small hairs on the bee's body. As the bee travels from flower to flower, the pollen falls onto new blossoms. This is called pollination.

Our fresh green plants have been touched by thoughtful tending.
With quiet patience we watched and wondered.
Now our veggies pop, pop, popping.
With great joy we are celebrating!

Tomorrow brings a tasty harvest.
Gently shines Mr. Moon's soft light.
Time to close our eyes and rest.
I bid you a sweet and peaceful night.

Terra Dot-to-Dot

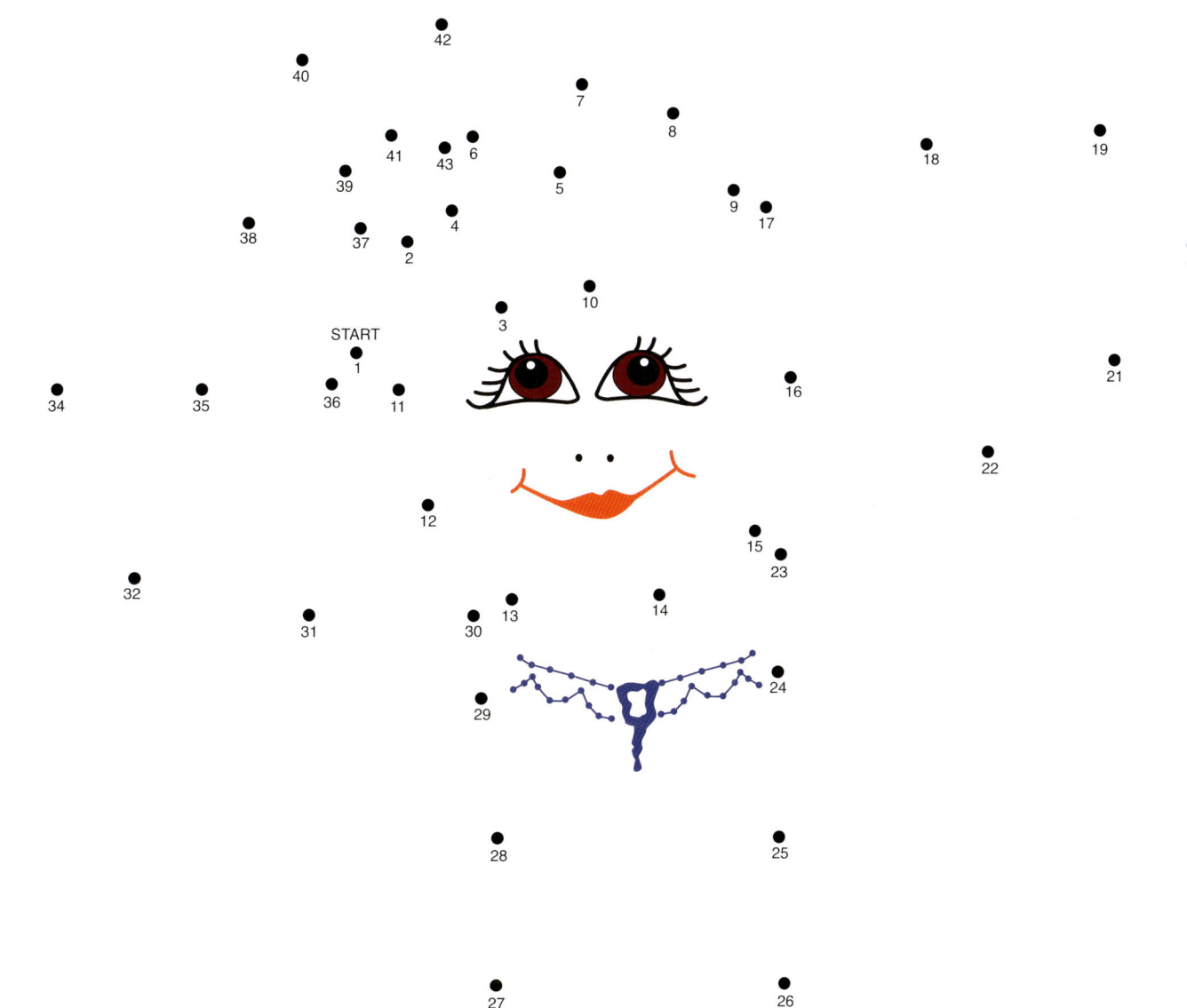

Time to harvest nature's treats.
Crisp, delicious, oh so neat!
Off we scamper with our pails.
Here we go along the trails.

First to pop is Razzy Radish.
Some taste sweet, some taste zesty.
Crisp and fresh,
and so sassy!

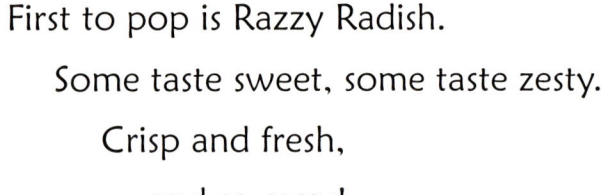

Yummy Luscious Linda Lettuce!
Make a sandwich for our lunch.
We'll munch our lettuce,
crunch,
crunch,
crunch!

Dear lovely Sweet Peas,
  weaving on the vine.
    They are a perfect snack that is so fine.

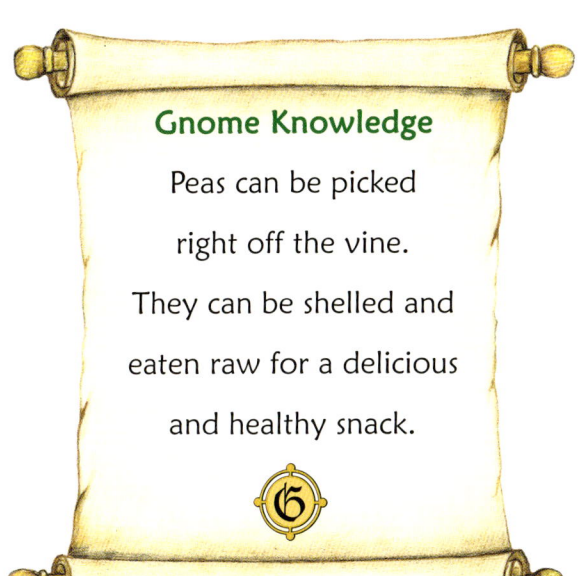

Gnome Knowledge

Peas can be picked right off the vine. They can be shelled and eaten raw for a delicious and healthy snack.

Big Ben Beans have grown so tall.
  Careful now, don't be quick.
    Be tender as you pluck and pick.

Carrots grow nice and deep,
shaped like a spinning top.
Bright and orange is this crop.

Nibbling on Silly Sally Spinach,
more and more is what I wish.
Cooked or fresh, a tasty dish!

Some days are made to plant.

Some days are made for harvest.

Summer days are almost gone.

Winter days are not for long.

Gerome and friends are quite content.
They are so glad they have been sent
to your home where they will stay
for when we plant another day.

Crickets chirping all around,
such a calm and lovely sound.
The evening fire is all aglow.
Time to relax and take it slow.

…Peace to all, and a gentle sweet night.

Know Your Gnome

(Circle the words you find.)

- Trellis
- Gerome
- Trowel
- Terra
- Bean
- Sweet Pea
- Lettuce
- Spinach
- Carrot
- Thelma Sue
- Radish
- Freddie
- Growing
- Seeds

```
T R E L L I S L L I E V
I B O W Z D V F L E R Z
B R G N A I O R B E A N
E J G E R O M E E Y D Y
Z U R P R R A D I A I N
T R O W E L S D M E S C
B O W Y T E H I R P H A
F G I V L T L E C T S R
S W N A D T Q L H E U R
E N G I J U U E I E N O
E S U S E C S O N W E T
D A X T H E L M A S U E
S P I N A C H L O I D S
```